Life Without Refrigeration

by
Susan Gregersen

Special thanks to

Steven
Emily and Stephen
David
Barbara
JD Smith

For their contributions to this project

Table of Contents

Introduction...7
Why would you ever be without refrigeration?...11
Why do some foods need to be kept cold...........13
Places to keep food cool................................15
    Root cellar..15
    Evaporative cooler....................................20
    Sand pots...23
    Snow cave...26
    Ice Houses..29
    Springs and wells.....................................39
    Basements and crawl spaces.......................45
Preserving: Canning, dehydrating, salting, etc.....47
Commercial dried and canned meat and dairy products...55
Commercial dried and canned alternatives to meat and dairy products.......................................61
Domestic dairy and meat animals.......................65
Extending food life (Don't spit in the jar!).........74
Conclusion..78

Introduction

According to a New York Times article I recently read, 99.5% of Americans own a refrigerator. I've lived without a refrigerator for most of the last thirty years, so I guess I'm among the 'unique' group of folks without one. For most of that time I've lived too far from the nearest grocery store to just make a quick convenience trip. It's usually more than half an hour's drive to the grocery store, and farther if I wanted cheap prices.

A lot of the people living without refrigerators that I talked to while researching this book live close enough to stores that they shop daily. For those who live or work in town and have daily access to a grocery store, this is a way to live without refrigeration without much impact on their lives. They had learned little things like keeping condiments in a cool, dark closet or pantry, and they knew that butter will keep outside of the fridge for about a week, depending on the ambient temperature of their kitchen.

Some of the people without refrigerators changed their eating styles to adapt to living without cold or frozen storage of food. Others kept a cooler and brought ice home from work or had ice packs like those little blue plastic packs, which they froze in a freezer belonging to friends or relatives.

Those are all ways to live without running a refrigerator in your home, but it's not quite what I mean by 'life without refrigeration'. Over my years of no refrigeration I learned ways to preserve foods usually refrigerated, and found sources to buy the things I couldn't preserve myself. I also learned about different ways to cool foods, such as evaporative cooling, and which foods could be stored that way.

We live 'off grid', meaning we don't have a power line connected to our home. When we bought our home here in NW Montana it was three miles to the nearest power line, and the power company wanted $27,000 to run a power line to us. Since then, over the last ten years, a couple of the neighbors have run power and now the nearest power line is only a mile away. But for less than $10,000 we eventually put in a solar power set-up that we are quite happy with.

Most of our neighbors had or have a propane refrigerator, and that was an option for us. But we chose not to. Instead, we dug a root cellar and learned of other ways to live without refrigeration. In other places where we lived we had other options available to us for cooling food. For example, when we lived in Kentucky we had a water-tight jug which we put food inside of and sunk in a cold water spring, and in Nevada we used evaporative cooling to keep food cool.

These alternatives are safe with some foods, but not with others. I'll talk about that in this book, as well as other aspects of food safety as it relates to refrigeration.

I'm not an expert. I'm just a regular person sharing what I learned along the way. I've also included stories from people who live or have lived without refrigeration.

Why would you ever be without refrigeration?

There are a lot of reasons why this could happen. It could be voluntary, such as moving to an off-grid property or choosing to give up your refrigerator.

Or it could be involuntary, such as the electric power grid going down due to a natural disaster or terrorist/war act.

Perhaps your refrigerator will quit working at a time when you can't afford to replace it. It's a purchase that can hit you when you least expect it and have few reserves to fall back on.

Maybe you want to lower your electric bills, and maybe you want to find ways to reduce your impact on the planet.

Whether it's voluntary or involuntary, it usually involves a lot of life changes or a lot of frantic work to preserve the food from a refrigerator or freezer. You might think "Oh, I'll throw a big party and invite everyone in the neighborhood", but if it's a community-wide power outage everyone else might have the same idea!

If it's just *your* fridge that went out, then the party idea might be a good hit!

At any rate, it's a good idea to have some back-up plans and information, just in case.

Why do some foods need to be kept cold

Refrigeration is basically a process to put food into suspended animation. The cold temperatures create an environment which slows the growth of bacteria that can spoil food. Freezing food does this on a more extreme scale, often stopping the growth of bacteria altogether until the food is thawed. During refrigeration the growth doesn't stop but it slows enough to allow you time to use the food while it is still 'good'; in other words, still safe to eat. That is why the food will eventually spoil, even in the refrigerator, if you don't use it.

Some foods, such as many condiments, contain vinegar, which also slows the growth of bacteria. These foods don't need to be kept as cold, however if you do keep them in the refrigerator, they will last much longer than if you store them in a pantry or closet or other non-refrigerated location.

Foods such as meat and milk will generally spoil very quickly if not kept cold, and I mean *cold* as in just above freezing. There are processes for meat and dairy products to keep them from spoiling as quickly, such as smoke-curing or brining meats, making jerky, or making butter or cheese from dairy products. The growth of bacteria is slowed by those processes, but they may still need to be refrigerated. They will last longer than fresh, unprocessed meat or milk, in most cases.

Nowdays most smoking or curing of meats is done for flavor rather than preserving, but the theory is still the same. There are some differences in the processes, so be sure you know what you're doing. Some of that will be covered later in this book, and I'll give resources for more information.

Places to keep food cool

Root cellar

One of the first things we did when we bought our current home is to dig a root cellar. We didn't have much money and couldn't hire a backhoe, so my husband and sons dug it by hand. My husband would break up the dirt with a pick and the boys would shovel it out. When they had a hole that was about 6' by 8', and about 6' deep, they chopped out an entry 'trench' down into the hole. The ground is stable here, so the sides didn't try to cave into the hole.

Then they laid logs across the top, side by side, all the way across the hole, making sure at least a foot of the log was sitting on solid dirt on each end. They also laid a couple of old, solid wooden doors across the logs, then a layer of 6-mil plastic.

Next they shoveled about a foot of dirt over the top, another layer of plastic, then the rest of the dirt was heaped over it. An old wooden door was laid over the access trench and simply removed to allow entry into the root cellar. The only expense for the root cellar was the roll of plastic from Home Depot. It was labor intensive, though, and took a couple weeks to build, since my husband also had a full-time job. Our sons were 14 and 16 during the construction of the root cellar.

We have the book "Root Cellaring" by Mike and Nancy Bubel, which is THE book for learning about building root cellars and similar cool storage areas. We'd read in the book about putting in proper venting, but we didn't have anything to use for the vents, and we didn't know how to keep the root cellar dry and still put in vents. It still doesn't have vents, even though we know, now, how we could have done it, and we have plastic pipe laying around.

Food keeps very well in our primitive root cellar. It's damp in there, so we don't store anything metal in there. We put some home-canned food in there the first winter and the lids rusted. Now we stick to fresh food like potatoes and carrots, and food stored in plastic buckets or containers. Potatoes and carrots keep clear into the next summer in the root cellar. Our climate here in northwest Montana is cool. Even in summer when our days get into the 80s and 90s, it drops to 40 or colder at night. Pine trees also shade the root cellar, keeping the sun from heating the ground.

In the first couple years we stored onions and squash down there. The onions rotted quickly, and now we store them in a cardboard box in a back bedroom of our cabin. The squash lasted a little longer than the onions in the root cellar, but it lasts all winter in the same back bedroom we store the onions in now. Primarily we keep potatoes, carrots, grains (in sealed plastic buckets), and paint cans in the root cellar. Modern paint cans are plastic, so they don't rust like metal cans. It's also the only storage area we have that doesn't freeze in winter, which is why we move any paint cans we have, to the root cellar in the fall.

Our root cellar stays around 40 degrees year round. If we have temperatures below zero for a few days, or long cloudy spells barely above zero, it's dropped as low as 36. In summer it's climbed as high as 45 in August, but most years it doesn't get that warm. We used to keep gallon jugs of water in the root cellar to use for making "iced tea", since all of our other water was room temperature, and in July and August that can be 90 degrees.

We don't have a well, so there's no opportunity to let the water run until it's cold. When it's hot outside, that 40-degree water from the root cellar tasted very refreshing.

We kept condiments in the root cellar, as well as butter and cheese. We placed the butter and cheese in plastic containers, usually the 32-oz. yogurt cartons, or the quart-sized potato salad 'buckets'. That way we didn't have trouble with mice or bugs getting into it. Since the walls are dirt it was easy for those critters to get in there. We've never have a lot of trouble with them though.

My husband build wooden boxes and drilled dozens of holes in all four sides for ventilation, and we store the potatoes and carrots in them. The holes are small, about ¼ inch or smaller, so mice can't get into the boxes and chew up our garden produce.

The root cellar is also a great place to store extra bottles and jars of cooking oil, peanut butter, shortening, and dehydrated foods. The cold, dark environment extends their shelf life.

Evaporative cooler

In arid climates you can make a cold box that'll be at least 20 degrees cooler than the surrounding air. We've done this in southern Nevada. It can be as simple as a wet towel placed over the food, to a fancy box covered in screening with a cloth cover and a water hose dripping onto the cloth to keep it wet.

We used a small cake pan with a cereal bowl in the middle. We put a package of cheese and two sticks of butter in the bowl. Then we poured water in the cake pan up to about halfway up the cereal bowl and laid a dishcloth over the bowl with the cheese, tucking the bottoms of the cloth into the water of the cake pan. That caused the dish towel to wick up water and kept it wet. I laid a small thermometer in with the cheese, and an hour later it was 52 degrees under the towel and the surrounding air temperature was in the upper 70s. I kept it in the shade and we stored cheese, butter, and condiments like that for several days. This was during a desert camp-out.

At the library in Searchlight, Nevada there is a small museum. One of the things we saw there in 2011 was an evaporative cooling box. It was about 2 1/2' tall and a foot and a half wide, and about 2' front to back. The box was framed with 2" by 2" boards and covered with 1/2" hardware cloth, which is also called hail screen in some places. Hardware cloth is like metal window screen only the holes are bigger than screen, in this case, half an inch. It's tougher, like fencing.

There was a cloth cover over it and a small hose dripped water onto the top. This was sitting outside on the sand, so they didn't have anything under it to catch any water that might drip. The front opened like a refrigerator door. This type of set-up is usually safe for foods that don't have to be kept as cold. I wouldn't keep milk or meat in one, but I would comfortably keep cheese, butter, ketchup, mayo, and mustard in it. Safety-conscious people would probably cringe, but unless the weather was really hot I'd store leftovers in it overnight.

Sand pots

I've heard mixed reports of whether this actually works well. Some people swear it does, but others say it doesn't keep food cold enough. It may depend *what* you're trying to keep cold. Since some foods don't have to be kept as cold as others, this might be an excellent food-cooling method for those lesser-cold foods.

The way it works is that you take two pots, one about an inch bigger overall, and you filled the layer between the pots with wet sand. Any type of sand is okay. The food is placed inside the smaller pot and a wet towel goes over it, tucked in on the wet sand between the pots.

One of my friends uses two porous ceramic planter pots, and the other friend says you have to have a non-porous outer container. The second friend uses a plastic or metal pot for the outside, and a porous pot for the inner pot. It seems the porous inner pot is the important item.

Pour water into the sand from time to time as it evaporates. Both of my friends say to just keep the sand damp. I did a google search on this and none of the sites I looked at said if it was a problem to over-fill the wet sand layer, but everyone agrees that you shouldn't let the sand dry out.

If possible, put a thermometer inside the inner pot and monitor the temperature for a while. Only put in foods that store safely at cool temperatures, not foods that need cold temperatures until you know whether it's cold enough to be safe for the foods that require a lower temperature.

A friend of mine, J.D. Smith, wrote to me recently: "*I do know a bit about refrigeration in a SHTF situation. For a dry location, get two clay pots. One large, one small enough to fit in the large on, giving at least one inch of room around the inside and top. Soak the pots in cool water. Get some sand and wet it down as well. Put a little wet sand in the bottom of the large pot. Put the small pot in the large*

Ice Houses

In places where ponds and lakes freeze in the winter you can make an Ice House, also known as an Ice Cellar or an Ice Cave, and store blocks of ice in it. When properly built the ice can last all summer.

When I was a child my Grandma had an ice cellar under her barn. There was a trapdoor next to the stall where she milked her cow and we always asked if we could see what was down there. One time she did open the trapdoor so we could look.

Wooden stairs descended into a dank, dark room lit by one lightbulb hanging from the side of the steps. It had been cleaned of sawdust but I don't remember what the floor was made of. I only remember the smelly cement walls.

The cellar hadn't been used for years. By that time my Grandma had a refrigerator and didn't use the ice cellar any more. This was in the 1960s.

My Dad told us how they cut the ice with a long saw with big teeth. They made a hole in the ice and put the saw through the hold and cut blocks about two feet by two feet, and whatever thickness the ice was. They made test holes to check the thickness before they started cutting, and in northwestern Wisconsin the ice often got two feet thick or more.

After the block was cut they attached tongs to it. A rope ran from the tongs to their team of horses and the horses would pull the block up and across the lake. They cut several blocks and loaded them onto a wagon to take to the barn. There was a pulley on the ceiling of the barn so that they could lower the ice into the cellar.

The cellar floor was lined with sawdust and the blocks were stacked on the sawdust. Sawdust was packed around and over each block as it was put in the cellar. I always thought it was for insulation to help keep the ice blocks from melting but shortly before he died, when we were talking about ice houses, my Dad said the sawdust's other job was to keep the ice blocks from sticking together. As they melted they would fuse themselves together and they were hard to get apart if there wasn't something like sawdust to keep the blocks apart.

One old farm we visited at some point in my youth had a cave dug into the hill. It had collapsed in on itself but I pointed to it and said "Oh, a root cellar!" and my Dad said it had been an ice cave. He had seen it when he was a child. They had dug into the side of a hill and shored it up with boards, and lined it with sawdust and kept their ice in there. We poked around and there was a rotted mess of sawdust and old splintered boards in there.

Once upon a time it had a door on it, and the remains of it showed it was a two-door thickness with insulation between the two doors. The doors were attached to each other and opened together. My Dad said sometimes they filled the doors with sawdust for insulation.

The generation of people who know about ice houses from real life experience is fading as they pass away. A good place to find out about ice houses and other old-time things is to visit a nursing home. The people there love to talk about the 'old days' and you can pick up a lot of knowledge and tips from them. But go soon! Every day we lose more of our treasure of old knowledge as one here and then one there passes away.

I've seen plans in modern publications about how to build an above-ground ice house. They usually involve a very insulated building, often with double walls that are filled in between with sawdust, hay, wood chips, or other natural/organic insulating material. Interestingly I have never seen plans for an ice house that involved store-bought modern insulating material such as fiberglass or styrofoam. I know of someone who built an above ground "root cellar" using cement blocks and sheets of styrofoam insulation, but I've never seen an ice house built that way.

Basically the above-ground ice house is a very well insulated shed where you store blocks of ice. Sawdust is the main thing used to pack around, between, and above the ice blocks, but if a person can't get sawdust in that sort of quantity they could try tightly packing hay or straw around it. It might not work as well as sawdust but at least you tried something. Leaves tightly packed, especially when they get crumbly, might also work.

In the old days everyone cut wood for their stoves and sawdust was in abundance. There were also sawmills around in northern Wisconsin where my Dad grew up, and here where we live now in northwestern Montana the older people talk about getting sawdust from the local mills. In the Fall they would clean out the ice houses/cellars/caves and pile the old sawdust to compost for the garden.

As you remove the blocks be sure the surrounding blocks are covered with sawdust or whatever material you used.

We played with freezing our own blocks of ice one winter, even though we don't have an ice house (yet!). In our climate we can freeze a block solid in a couple days during cold spells. Unfortunately the 'blocks' we froze were actually cylinders, frozen in rubber bowls meant for feeding and watering animals. We used those because they don't break like plastic buckets will when water expands as it freezes.

If you want to make your own blocks of ice you might want to find a way to make your own 'molds' for freezing them. I've tossed ideas around in my head and the closest I've come in my imagination is wooden boxes lined with plastic sheeting. However the plastic sheeting, which is to prevent water leaking out through the cracks between the boards, would have to be replaced often. Cold makes plastic brittle and it would tear easily.

You can buy plastic sheeting at home-building centers in 100-foot rolls but if the world were to economically collapse or go to war or fall apart in any other way, you would not be able to replace the plastic sheeting. So you'd want to devise a plan for making blocks that fit with what you anticipate for the future.

For myself the plan would most likely involve something I didn't need outside resources to replace. I don't like spending money I don't have to spend if I can come up with a different way to do it. But so far the only way I know to do it involves the rubber buckets and cylindrical and slightly-tapered ice blocks, which would be a bit harder to stack safely than square blocks. Now that I think about it I could lay them on their sides, pack them well with sawdust, and keep stacking them, using the surrounding walls to keep them from rolling all over the place.

When you cut or make your ice blocks think about how you will use them. If you plan to put them in a cooler like the way ice blocks purchased at the store are sometimes used by people going camping, you'll want to cut (or make) your ice blocks small enough to fit.

In the old days they had "ice boxes", which varied a lot in style. My Grandma had an old ice box on her back porch that she didn't use any more. It resembled a refrigerator except that hers was about 4-feet high and it sat on a small table that raised it about two feet off the floor. It had a shelf near the top where the block of ice sat. They used a "half-cake", or half of a block, which fit just fine in the tray. There was a tube that came out of it and ran down and out the bottom of the ice box, and as the ice melted the water ran through that. I'm not sure where the water went but I'm guessing they set a bucket under the table the ice box sat on, and it caught the water.

You can get creative in making a cooler or box but be sure you allow for the melting water. If worse comes to worse, you can put the ice and food in the bathtub and cover it with towels or blankets. The damp towels and blankets would also work to help keep the food cool as the water evaporated off the cloth. The excess water from the melting ice would go down the drain. An old washtub on legs with a drain hose is another option. Or now that I think about it...if the power is out anyway, you could use your wash machine. It would be awkward to put the food and ice in there, but it would work.

The ice boxes didn't keep as cold as modern refrigerators but they were better than nothing and they kept the foods stored back in those days adequately cold. The typical refrigerator of the 'old days' contained a much different collection of food than the modern refrigerator in the typical house. Back then fruits and vegetables were often stored in a root cellar or just in a back room. Now you'll find them in refrigerators along with many bottles of condiments, salad dressings, etc.

My Grandma's fridge in the 1960's didn't have soda pop, dozens of condiments, plastic containers of leftovers, cartons of yogurt or cream cheese, marinades and other sauces. However a lot of those things would have kept well in an ice box because those are foods that don't require as cold a temperature as meat and milk.

Certainly my Grandma kept milk in her ice box, but she milked a cow daily until she was in her 80s (and I was in my teens) and used it in everything. I can't remember for sure but I guess she was using fresh milk each day. I know that when she had excess milk (like when we weren't around to drink it up) she would make cottage cheese and feed it to the chickens. She said the calcium was good for them.

A lot of things were made fresh as she went, which was typical in that day. It would be a good idea to learn how to make your favorite things from scratch, or at least to have the recipes on hand. Things like mayo are easy to make. Right now a lot of us feel too busy to make things fresh as we go, but if the SHTF we might have more time to do so, since we wouldn't be running off to jobs and soccer practices and shopping. However, I'd much rather that *not* happen because I would like to see my grandkids grow up in a stable world where they can just buy a jar of mayo if they don't want to make their own.

Springs and wells

If you are among the lucky, you have a spring on or near your property, and it's a cold spring. I could see the pleasure of having a hot spring and being able to make a pool to soak in, but if you're in need of non-refrigerator food-cooling, a cold spring trumps the hot spring.

When we lived in southeast Kentucky there were springs bubbling out all over the mountainside. Our house had a well but the pump went out and we didn't have the money to buy a new one, so we bought cheap garden hoses from Wal-mart and ran them up to a spring above the house.

I bought two plastic colanders/food strainers, which look like bowls with holes for draining water off of food, and I wired them together to make a ball. Then I made a small hole in the side and put the intake end of the garden hose in that and secured it with duct tape and string. It made a dandy filter to keep leaves and debris out of the hose.

I sunk the colander ball into the small pool where the spring came out of the rock, and the water flowed down the hose to the house. I screwed the other end to the outside spigot on the house and opened the valve. We then had running water, although with weak pressure. But still...it was water and we didn't have to haul it in a bucket or jug.

I kept food in that small pool too. We had electricity up there, sort of. The power line ran from a meter half a mile away at the bottom of the hill, and the line was strung on branches and bushes and even on the ground in some places. We didn't own the home and the owner was letting us live there for free, so we didn't complain. The house was nice, it was just lacking in amenities!

By the time the power got to the house it was too weak to run a refrigerator. It was too weak to power the microwave or stove. About all we could power was the lights and a few small things. We had a small TV and a Super-nintendo for the kids. There was no TV reception back in those hills, but the kids could play video games.

We dug a cave by hand into the hill behind the house. It was small but just right to put a cooler in there, about 2' long and 18" front-to-back. I set a kitchen table in the 'cave' for structural support, used boards along the legs to create a "wall" around the sides and back, and we back-filled with the dirt we dug out, and piled the rest up around the outside.

We walked a mile and a half down off the mountain to attend a small mission church, where I played the piano, twice a week. They let us keep gallon milk jugs of ice in the freezer in the kitchen. We had three sets of two jugs going. One would be in the cooler. One would have been taken out of the cooler and waiting until we walked down off the mountain again. And the third set was in the freezer at the church. We'd carry that second set, the melted ones, down the mountain and after church we'd put them in the freezer and carry the frozen ones back up to our house and put them in the cooler, taking out the ones that were in the cooler.

But getting back to "springs and wells", we also kept food in the little pool by the spring. I had a plastic gallon jar with a screw-on lid, and I put cheese and butter and things like that which would fit, into the jar and put it in the pool. I weighted it down with a large flat rock. Sometimes it would still tip over and the rock would slide off, and I'd find the jar floating half on it's side, but the food was still cold. I never tried storing milk or meat in it. We used powdered milk and canned meat. This was in the 1990s, not the old days.

Sometimes old-timers built springhouses, which are a small shed built over the source of the spring. I've been in a few at historical sites. They made a trough out of wood or cement, and the cold spring water ran through that. It was shallow, and food in crocks was set in the water. It didn't cover over them, and the flow was slow enough that it didn't wash them along the trough. The constant flow of cold water kept the food chilled.

It's likely the spring water wasn't cold enough to safely store meat, but I'm betting they stored milk in it for at least a day safely. I'm not sure how today's pasteurized and homogenized milk would store in cold spring water, but if you try it, drink it within a day. At that point in civilization (or the lack of it) you'd probably be milking your own cow or goat, or bartering for local milk, anyway.

There aren't as many open, hand-dug wells nowadays as in the old days, but if things fall apart, there may again be hand-dug wells where the water table is shallow enough. I'm not advocating them because they are dangerous to dig and dangerous to have around. But if you have one or have to dig one, the air down near the water is cold. People used to lower a bucket on a rope and suspend it a foot or so over the water, with their cold food inside the bucket.

I saw a hand-dug well that was lined with blocks of stones, and they had built it a shelf made of a flat stone sticking out from the wall, and they would lower their bucket onto that shelf. The rope was tied at the top to the support for the windlass. With the 'food' bucket to the side, the water bucket could still be raised and lowered to fetch water.

More comments from my friend, J.D. Smith: "*If you have a deep open well, put what you want to keep cool into a bucket on a rope. Secure the rope and put it down the well, making sure that you don't hit the water in the well. It should be above the water. Most people don't have an open well, so a spring house was another way to keep food. Spring water is very cold and will keep your things cold. The spring house does not need to be very big. A four by four by three feet is big enough.*"

Basements and crawl spaces

Basements and crawl-spaces can be used like root cellars. They don't get cold enough, generally, to keep meat and dairy products, other than properly stored dairy products like butter and cheese. The exception is in extremely cold weather when a crawl space can freeze. In those cases you need to make sure you remove any fruits or vegetables so they don't freeze.

Depending on the reason for your refrigerator being out, and the time of year, basements and crawl spaces can be good places to temporarily put foods other than milk or meat. Be sure they are in containers that will protect them from rodents, insects, or water.

My neighbor, Barbara, who also lives without refrigeration, wrote to me: _"During the long, cold winter we put food against the coldest wall, which is near our north-facing front door, and cover it with blankets_ *to insulate it against the heat of the house. The food doesn't keep as long as it would in a fridge, and meat is a definite no-no unless it will be used the same day. Things like ketchup and Parmesan cheese seem to last forever this way."*

Our family has stored food against a back door and covered it with towels or blankets. In the winter months this works quite well. We've had things freeze there, such as a carton of cottage cheese. But then in our cabin we've had things freeze that were stored underneath beds in the back rooms.

Preserving: Canning, dehydrating, salting, etc.

You can make use of these food preserving techniques to keep meat and dairy products on hand. The finished product often isn't the same fresh. Milk, for example, comes out looking and tasting like commercially-canned evaporated milk. I don't know how they commercially 'can' milk in those cardboard cartons and have them come out so close to fresh milk, but in my home canning I end up with brownish-yellow milk that has a 'canned' taste to it. It's still a drinkable product, just not the same as fresh. (Check into dehydrating milk)

Cheese can be canned or dried at home, as well as preserved by wax. Canning cheese is simple. My method is to cut the cheese into cubes and place in sterilized jars. Meanwhile I have the lids (or caps, depending where you live and what you call them) in a small pan, covered with water and simmering to soften the rubber

sugar or vinegar, and eaten within a couple weeks. These and other methods are covered more in-depth in the book "Food Storage: Preserving Meat, Dairy, and Eggs".

My friend, J.D. Smith, makes her own cheese and waxes them for preservation: "

"Waxing cheese is not difficult, its as simple as melting and dipping or brushing it on to the cheese. Some dip, some brush and some do both. Brushing takes practice. Dipping is easy. If you are going to try to brush use a natural bristle brush. A synthetic brush will melt.

Find an old pot because you will not be able to use it for anything else. Get a pot a little bigger so you can set the wax pot into it. You want to put water into the bigger pot and just simmer the water. put the small pot with the wax into the bigger one. Like a double boiler. Wax has a low flash point What that means is it can catch fire easily. Make sure you don't boil the water! You must watch the pot!

The cheese must be cold before you start to wax. Put it in the refrigerator. The wax sticks much better when cold. Make sure the cheese is dry before you start.

Once the wax has melted, dip the brush in the wax and start at the top. Brush a thin layer on and let it dry. Once dry Brush wax on the side and let it dry. Don't try to rush the drying. Once the side is dry do the bottom. If you are brushing you will need to put 4 or 5 layers on. Make sure the cheese is covered in the wax. If you leave even a small spot open unwanted bacteria will get in and spoil your cheese.

Dipping is easier and faster. Once the wax is melted dip the top of the cheese in the wax. Let it dry and do the same for the bottom as well as the sides. When doing the side roll it in the wax putting your fingers on the top and bottom so as to not burn your fingers or hand. Be careful the wax is very hot.

What wax to use: Cheese wax is the best.

It comes in red, yellow, and black. You can find it in specialty shops or online. You can also use beeswax. Cheese wax and beeswax are very pliable which is what you want. It wont crack and let nasty bacteria in.

Please don't use candle wax not only is it not pliable it can crack and let unwanted bacteria in and spoil your cheese. Never use a hard wax, including paraffin."

If you cut a piece off and are going to eat the rest within a week to ten days, then you don't re-wax it. The cheese will get a rind on it. Just cut off another piece and cut off the rind. If you plan on keeping it longer than stated, then you would take off the wax and re-wax the whole cheese.

We eat a lot of cheese, so one pound of it would last about 3 or 4 day. If you don't eat that much, then I would cut the cheese into what size you would eat in a week, and wax it in those sizes."

<u>Commercial dried and canned meat and dairy products</u>

Canned meats and powdered milk are widely available. People who are used to fresh milk tend to think that powdered milk is icky. It does take some getting used to, and some people never get beyond using it in baking or on cereal, rather than drinking it. Some things can make it better. If you can use cold milk, it helps the flavor. Instant milk dissolves right away and it ready to use, but non-instant should be made up at least a few hours ahead of time, and chilled if possible. I prefer to keep instant powdered milk on hand, just for the convenience of not having to think ahead of time and mix up the non-instant milk.

You can buy milk in quart-size and smaller waxed cardboard cartons that don't have to be refrigerated until opened. A family could use it up quickly, though an individual would have to be willing to drink or use a lot of milk, if refrigeration or cooling of some kind wasn't available.

However, this could be a good option for a short-term storage plan, such as for emergencies or disasters.

If it's going to be a lifestyle for you, to not have a refrigerator, this is still an option but it's going to cost more than the electricity to run a refrigerator and buying low-priced dairy products and meats.

Tips from a Neighbor

The following is a few tips and ideas about freeze-dried butter, milk, and eggs from a young woman, Barbara, who lives off-grid without refrigeration near our home. She and her husband left the city two years ago and built a small cabin out here in the woods. As new as they are to the lifestyle, they knew of a few things I didn't. The following is more of a review on a few products she uses:

"I use Augason Farms Butter Powder in place of real butter of margarine, since we don't have a refrigerator to keep things like butter in. I've used it in cooking and

baking, and the results are excellent. In fact, this butter powder is so superior to fresh butter that if I had a fridge I'd still be using it. It is a somewhat thickish powder and is measured similar to real butter in that 1/2 cup of butter is 1/2 cup of butter powder. You only need 1 1/2 teaspoons of water to make it usable.

This seems like an awful small amount of water compared to how much powder you're using, but it does come together after a bit of mixing. Since I've started using it in my baking it's improved it a lot. I have never had cookies or cakes come out this good before.

The powder is also very convenient. You never have the "oops" moment of starting a recipe only to notice you forgot to set the butter out to soften up. You never have to deal with the melted mess of trying to soften it in a microwave. You never wind up with a stick that's half-melted, half-solid from setting it on a woodstove for a bit. No chunks you're trying to mash up with a fork. Just a simple bit of powder and a bit of water. There is no taste difference, though I've noticed a difference in smell if I use it in cooking. There is a quality difference, and to me, butter powder wins.

I've also used the augason Farms Scrambled Egg Mix as well as EnerG Egg Replacer. Egg replacer is safe to eat if you're interested in eating raw cookie dough. I'd not an exact egg replacer, nutritionally, and it says so on the box. It does act like eggs by replacing the leavening and binding usually brought about by eggs in a recipe when you are baking. I have even used egg replacer in meat loaf. The box has directions for how to mix if you want just the whites. The Egg Replacer is nice if you are cutting a large recipe in half and wind up with it calling for half an egg.It's mixed with 1 1/2 teaspoons egg replacer powder to 2 tablespoons water for one egg, so you can easily cut that in half to equal half an egg.

The scrambled egg mix from Augason farms can be used in baking as well. I recently made a cake using it. It looked really weird going into the oven with chunks of egg mix floating in the batter, but it came out really nice. Moist, springy, and produced one of my better cakes. I have also used the Egg Mix for scrambled eggs and omelets. My only complaint is that it is chunky. I've started mixing the mix in a separate container with an egg beater because it's so chunky.

Milk powder is a definite must. When using it for cold cereal I never measure it exactly. I just pour water into the bowl, then add powder until it looks right. Otherwise it's 1/3 cup powder to one cup of water, to make one cup of milk. If recipe calls for, say, 3/4 cup of milk I take my 1/3 measure and fill it 3/4 of the way full. The only thing is that it only comes in non-fat, which doesn't bother me. I think they do make a whole milk version but as far as I know, it's hard to find. Seems to me if you wanted to make it taste "thicker" you'd just add a little more powder than it calls for."

I've never used the butter powder from Augason farms, and I'm not sure which company she gets the milk powder from, but I have used the Augason farms scrambled egg mix. I haven't had the same problem as Barbara has. I mix the scrambled egg mix into the dry ingredients of a cake mix and stir it thoroughly before adding the wet ingredients and I've never seen yellow bits of egg in the cake batter. We've cooked the eggs as scrambled eggs for breakfast and also had them come out good. We usually stir things like onions, peppers, bacon bits, etc., into our scrambled eggs as we cook them, so possibly it hides the chunks, if they're there.

She is right though. It makes excellent cakes that rise higher than with fresh eggs and have a great moist texture. I've also used the EnerG Egg Replacer she talks about, but I think it makes a drier cake and harder cookies than the scrambled egg mix.

Commercial dried and canned alternatives to meat and dairy products

I bet this looks like the same chapter you just read. But there's one word that's different. "Alternatives". People who are vegans or vegetarians have used these product and others for years. Some people are like me and can't digest dairy products.

Shopper beware! Some of the products labeled as "Milk alternative" do contain dairy products. Honeyville, which is a company I respect and order from, carries an "instant milk alternative" in both regular and chocolate. They're made with whey and milk solids. READ the ingredients on any product you are considering buying. Sometimes they're hidden down in the list and sometimes they have funny names, so make sure you're aware of all the various terms that are used for foods you're sensitive to or allergic to. Most foods have an allergy notice stating if it contains the most common allergens such as wheat, dairy, soy, nuts, etc., but read the ingredients list yourself!

Most of the milk substitutes, such as soy, rice, coconut, or almond milk, come in quart-sized or half-gallon waxed cardboard cartons. They're usually shelf-stable until opened, then need to be kept cool after opening. A quart-sized carton would be easy for most people to use up in a day, so it's not likely to spoil before it's used up.

Powdered non-milks are also available. "Better Than Milk" rice milk powder is made by Tofutti. They also make powdered "fake" sour cream and "fake" cream cheese.

In the old days Loma Linda and other companies made canned 'meat alternatives'. There was a ground meat/hamburger made of TVP, 'fake' chicken nuggets (these were *really* good!), and non-meat hot dogs. The non-meat hot dogs were so good I preferred them to the real thing.

I haven't seen these canned non-meats in years. But nowdays dried TVP is widely available, already flavored for beef or chicken, and sometimes seasoned as "Mexican-flavored TVP" or "Italian TVP" and others. It comes in crumbles and in chunks. Our local grocery store has a selection of Augason Farms Freeze-dried foods, which includes the #10 cans of flavored TVP.

We can also order it through our local food-buying co-op, which orders from a company in Oregon called "Azure Standard". They deliver all over the northwest and much of the Pacific coast. If you ask at your local health food store they might know of a similar company to order from.

On an internet search I found these sites that carry these foods:

usaemergencysupply.com
healthy-eating.com
thereadystore.com
harmonyhousefoods.com
wholefoodsmarket.com
augasonfarms.com

I recently bought a can of the Augason Farms beef-flavored TVP in a #10 can, and I used some to make a "fake beef" and vegetable soup. It was very good. Other than the texture being slightly different that roast beef, it was hard to tell the difference. One of our daughters used some to make chili. She and her husband both said it was every bit as good as 'real meat'. We all use either beef or venison for things like soup and chili, so we're used to a variation in the taste of 'meat'.

Domestic dairy and meat animals

If you have the land and the time, it can be a great experience and add wholesome meat and dairy products to your diet. Let's start with dairy animals.

First off, decide what it is you want from your dairy animal. Do you want to be able to make butter? Or cheese? It's difficult to separate the cream in goat's milk without an electric separator (difficult doesn't mean impossible), so if butter is important to you, cow's milk is a better option. The cream separates itself and you just have to carefully skim it off the top.

If cheese is of interest to you, goat's milk turns out some really good cheeses. Goats also take less space and feed than cows. There are more dairy goats on individual and family farms than there are dairy cows. More people worldwide drink goat milk than cow milk. As a matter of interest, there are also places where sheep's milk is consumed as much as goat's milk. It's less common in the United States but I do know a couple in our area who have sheep for milk, meat, and wool. They switched from goats to sheep because sheep are "less troublesome and easier to contain in a pen" than goats.

Feed is an important consideration. If the "SHTF", how would you feed your animals? Think about what and how much they eat now (if you already have them, and if you don't, find these things out), and figure out how you'll grow or barter for them. You can't just look at a grassy field and say "I'll get a scythe and cut it myself and stack it like a haystack" because that won't be enough in northern climates with short growing seasons. And to produce milk, you're probably going to need some grain to supplement the grass or hay.

"But", you say, "the pioneers kept their animals fed on the prairie and remote places where they moved to". Yes, they did. But do you know how? Do you have the equipment they had, primitive as it was? Do you have the strength and endurance? If times get bad, we'll all develop more of that.

Animals need water. If the power is out, where will you haul water from? How will you haul that water? Can you use a truck or car and haul it in jugs or barrels? Or will you have to carry it in buckets for quite a distance?

In the winter the water will freeze (unless you're in a warm climate), and you'll have to chop a hole in the ice so the animals can reach the water, or haul fresh water several times a day. We use multiple rubber buckets and bring them in the house to thaw, then rotate them. When we bring a frozen one in to thaw we pack snow in it as tightly as we can, to add more 'water' to the bucket.

We don't have a well. We collect rainwater in the summer (still legal here) for the garden and animals. In the winter we melt snow for the animals, and we haul our drinking water year-round from seven miles away. It can get tedious in the winter to keep melting snow and changing out buckets. At one time we had horses, goats, pigs, turkeys, chickens, and ducks, plus dogs and cats. Now we just have chickens, a dog, and a cat.

Sheds and other buildings are easy to make, as are fences if you have a place to cut poles and posts, or the means to buy fencing, wire, or posts. If you have the other things figured out, such as feed and water, then you'd probably do okay with dairy animals.

Do your research and learn all you can about the care of these animals. Try to find other people who have the type of animal you're interested in and talk to them. Find out what kind of problems can arise, and learn about basic medical care for minor ailments, and who the nearest (and good at their job) veterinarian is. In bad times things would probably go back to barter, so don't assume you wouldn't have the means to treat your animal if it develops a problem or becomes injured.

If you're going to make cheese from your milk, learn how now, not when the SHTF. Most cheese is made using rennet, but these simple cheeses don't require rennet or fancy equipment or procedures, and anyone can do it. The following instructions were provided by avid-cheese maker, J D Smith:

"Soft cheese is easy to make. You will not need rennet to make these cheeses. All the cheeses must be put in a covered container in the refrigerator or some place cool. They will keep for 1 to 2 weeks. Once you have tasted these yummy cheeses they may not last the day.

With the exception of the Queso Blanco all are spreadable. The Queso Blanco is a solid cheese that does not melt. You can cut it up to put into soup or other dishes. Or you can roll the chunks in bread crumbs and fry them. (Susan's note: I'm going to try this! Yum! I love breaded cheese!)

You don't have to use cheese salt. You can use non-iodized table salt or no salt. Its up to you.

Soft cheese without rennet.:

Yogurt Cheese

1 qt yogurt
cheese salt

Get the yogurt to room temperature. Put the yogurt at room temperatur in a colander lined with butter muslin. Bring the corners up and tie it into a bag and hang to drain. Drain for 12 to 24 hrs to desired consistency. Remove from bag and add salt to taste.
You can add herbs if you like. Spread on anything that you like: bread, crackers, muffins.

Lemon cheese

1/2 Gallon whole milk
1/4 cup lemon juice

Heat the milk in a large pot to 190 degrees. Add the lemon juice and stir it well.

Cover the pot and let it sit for 15 min. If it does not set add a little more lemon juice until it does.

Pour the curds in a colander lined with cheese cloth. Tie up and let it drain in the bag for a few hours. Put in salt to taste.

Queso Blanco

1 gallon whole milk
1/4 cup vinegar

Heat in a large pot 1 gallon milk to 190 degrees. Stir it or it will scorch. Add a little vinegar at a time. The curds will separate from the whey. Pour the curds in a colander lined with cheese cloth. Tie up and let drain 4 to 5 hours."

Meat animals have a lot of the same requirements as dairy animals. Cows and large livestock need space and in some cases, shelter. They need food and water, which I covered a few paragraphs before this one. Their needs aren't much less than dairy animals. If you're raising the animal for meat you want it to have good growth. If you skimp on the feed, there will be less meat in the finished product.

I've included meat and dairy animals because they are an alternative to refrigerated meat. Farmers in the old days would butcher in the fall, and the meat would be smoked or salted, or in cold places like northwest Wisconsin where my Dad grew up, the meat was placed on top of the shed or in a box on stilts (to keep wild animals from getting it). Over the summer meat was primarily the occasional chicken they butchered and ate the same day, or fish from local water holes. Salt pork was available most of the year in some parts of the country, since the old way of making it kept it preserved without refrigeration.

An excellent book on those food-preserving processes is "Food Storage: Preserving Meat, Dairy, and Eggs", which I co-wrote with David Armstrong. I'm not just promoting it because I co-authored it, but because the information on old-time food preservation methods is good information to have.

Another book that will help you decide what and how much you need is "Food Self-Sufficiency: Reality Check", also written by me. I'm not just trying to promote my own books, but they really are helpful books, and in kindle form they are cheap. Print copies can be nice to have around when you can't access your kindle or computer.

Extending food life (Don't spit in the jar!)

One of the fastest ways to spoil your food is to introduce bacteria into it. Sure, no one actually spits into a jar of mayonnaise or jelly, but how many times have you licked the knife or spoon and stuck it back in the jar? You may think that since you licked off all the food and it 'looked' clean, that it's clean, but small amounts of saliva are still on the surface and millions of little bacteria can attach themselves to that mayo, jelly, or other food. This can lead it to quickly spoil.

I watched someone make peanut butter and jelly sandwiches for her entire family this past winter. She spread peanut butter on a slice of bread, licked the knife and stuck it in the jelly, spread the jelly on the bread, licked the knife, slapped another slice of bread on it and handed it to one of her kids. She then repeated this with the whole family. Spread, lick, spread, lick… A scene just asking for someone to get sick.

Besides me, I mean, and I was just watching!

If you want your food to last longer, both in and out of the fridge, be diligent with cleanliness. Use a separate utensil for each food, and you can just let it sit in the jar while you work your way around with the other food you're using. Then take each knife, spoon, or whatever utensil out of the jar and screw on the lid immediately. At this point, it's okay to lick them off and toss them in the sink if you want.

Keep the surfaces clean that you are cutting food or setting food on. Is that counter you just layed your slices of bread on clean? Just because it's dry doesn't mean that it's clean. I'm not big into sterilizing things or using antibacterial soaps, but if I'm not sure the counter or table are free of bacteria and other germs, I grab a plate or cutting board to lay the food on.

Ever drink straight out of the milk jug? Juice bottle? Two-liter pop bottle? Any time you put your lips on a container you are transferring bacteria from your lips to the container. The milk or other food/drink will spoil much quicker.

Don't lick off the lid from a carton of cool whip or yogurt or salsa or any other food. When you put the lid back on the container, the food may come in contact with the residual bacteria. Even if it doesn't the bacteria will grow on the inside of the lid. Yes, refrigeration *slows* the growth of bacteria, but like I wrote at the beginning of the book, it does not *stop* the growth of bacteria. And if you're using alternative methods of keeping food cooled, the temperatures might not be cold enough to slow the bacterial growth.

Be careful handling food like cheeses. When you open the package, try not to touch the inside of the package or the cheese, unless you have washed your hands well. I buy cheese in blocks and hold the cheese by the outside of the wrapper and slice off the size of chunk that I need. Cheese doesn't have to be kept as cold as meat and milk, but it will mold quickly if you touch the cheese with contaminated hands.

In times of emergency or disaster, clean water might be scarce, and keeping your hands clean will be difficult. So use caution handling food. The last thing you need at a time like that is to have anyone get sick, especially if accompanied by vomiting and diarrhea. Not only could it be hard to get medical attention, it could be hard to keep the person hydrated if water is already scarce.

I'd like to think that anyone reading this has already given thought to storing water or making sure you'll have a water source in times of disaster or emergency. I know if I don't mention it I'll get a lot of emails saying "But Susan, you didn't tell people they should store water so they don't have this problem". On the other hand, you may just be reading this book because you're considering a move off-grid and want to know how to have 'cold' foods on hand, or their equivalents.

Conclusion

I hope that if you ever find yourself without a working refrigerator that you're able to use some of the ideas and tips in this book. I know for many of you they are not new ideas.

My purpose was to assemble as many ideas and methods as I could into one book. I've found some here and some there, but never compiled in one place.

I'm sure there are many more. It's a big world out there, and refrigeration is a relatively new convenience.

I keep a blog for ideas like these, and other food storage and self-sufficiency subjects. If you have ideas to add to this, feel free to email them to me and I'll add them to the blog.

I don't make money off the blog and can't pay you, but I would send you your choice of one of my books free of charge, for a good post about other non-refrigeration ideas.

The blog is located at:

http://www.povertyprepping.blogspot.com/

To comment or ask questions directly to me, please email me at:

povertyprepping@yahoo.com

And now a word from David, my co-author for the preserving meat, dairy, and eggs book. He's my hero of the food-growing and food-preserving world and is fearless at experimenting in his kitchen (his "lab-oh-rah-tory") with any food preservation ideas any of us come up with!

"Sue, I just thought of something. Fruitcake, if made right, can be stored for months without refrigeration.

I have one (half of one anyway!) that I made around Thanksgiving (he wrote this in June) *and vacuum-sealed to see how long it would keep.*

Well, I forgot about it until I found the bad a few weeks ago. I opened the food-saver bag and looked for any signs that it had spoiled (none found), smelled it (a bit like stale bread crumbs), then tasted it.

It was still pretty good, seven months without refrigeration - not bad! It's sealed back up and on the table now where I won't forget about it again.   - David

15868423R00048